Trudy B_____
June 2007

Seal Song

Text by Brian Davies

Photographs by Eliot Porter

Introduction by Roger Caras

Preface by Ray Bradbury

A Studio Book
The Viking Press   New York

To Nicky and Toni,
who lost more than anyone for the seals

By the same author
Savage Luxury

First published in 1978 by The Viking Press
625 Madison Avenue, New York, N.Y. 10022
Published simultaneously in Canada by
Penguin Books Canada Limited

Library of Congress catalog card number: 78-69851
ISBN 0-670-62668-6

Text and black-and-white illustrations printed in
the United States of America
Set in Bodoni Book
Color illustrations printed in Japan

All the color photographs in this book were taken by
Eliot Porter, unless otherwise credited on page 73. All
black-and-white photographs were made by Mark Read.

Contents

Introduction
by Roger Caras

Shakespeare Asked It All

It is pretty much accepted, I think, that despite the abuse heaped upon it by inadequate actors, the single line from *Hamlet,* "To be or not to be, that is the question," may be the most profound line ever written for a player to speak. It is the universal query, the eternal wondering. Are we in fact to exist or are we not to survive? Like the ill-starred prince of Denmark, if we select the negative option the end will be our own doing. Individuals die naturally; societies and civilizations generally commit suicide.

There are men and women who have locked themselves to what we deem the natural world and who have opted for the positive response to Hamlet. We are to be!, they proclaim, and they define *we* as all life rather than as just a single species. Their cosmic view of life compels them and they act despite ridicule, threat, and assault, and that is what must attract us to them. They will risk all, for their faith in life and the living is total. They are possessed by what they possess—a conscience.

Eliot Porter is such a man, for his eye is keener than ours, and when he makes the shorthand notations of what his eyes see—those notations we call photographs—we look and we say, "Yeah! Wow! Right on!" We can thank heaven itself for allowing man to develop a technique by which the superior eye can externalize its experiences.

Brian Davies, too, is a different man. He feels things more deeply than some of the rest of us, and even more unusual than that is the compulsion he feels as a result. He knows the compelling urge not only to tell us what he feels is wrong but to set out, at any cost, to right as much of that wrong as he can get at.

Eliot Porter and Brian Davies are experts at "show and tell," and that, in hot rage, is what this book is. They are showing us and telling us about the condition we are in. That cannot be done without making us want to know what we have to do to put things right.

I have never discussed religion with either Eliot Porter or Brian Davies, although I have had the pleasure of knowing both of them. I think, though, looking at this book, I can tell something about their religious beliefs. I don't know what knee they kneel on, what if any church they go to, but I will bet they subscribe to my own faith—the faith of "Don't Hurt." For hurt is what they have seen, hurt is what they have recorded, and that hurt is what this book is about. Porter and Davies are against hurt and that is what my religion is about.

What does it cost a man to stand up against pain in our addled world? Brian Davies has been stormed by angry mobs who felt his speaking out against their hurting made him deserving of physical violence. In Quebec his life was threatened, and only the expert wielding of a forearm by a three-hundred-pound companion saved him from serious attack on one occasion. Brian Davies and Eliot Porter (and I) along with a group of newsmen who had gathered from all over the world were barricaded in a motel in Newfoundland for several days, and Brian's helicopters were impounded by a mob that paraded and roared invectives day and night. It took a flying wedge of Royal Canadian Mounted Police who had been flown hundreds of miles for the purpose to disperse the mob. The Mounties controlled the mob but not the courts. A local magistrate then passed judgment on Davies in a courtroom full of leering opponents.

Davies was jailed, mocked, fined, and denied the right to fly anywhere near the seal hunt. This mocking of Davies had as its purpose the blinding of the free press. Davies was the instrument.

To stand up against pain, shame, and waste in this time is often to stand alone, often to be mocked, sometimes to be threatened. No one who seriously subscribes to the faith of "Don't Hurt" can go very far along the road dictated by his conscience without encountering the risks. It goes with the job.

People like Eliot Porter and Brian Davies, I think, believe that there is a link so firmly welded that the pain they see is the pain they feel. To see pain and fear and not feel pain and fear is a dangerous separation, too wide a gap. Albert Schweitzer discussed that point in *Out of My Life and Thought*. He said, "The idea of reverence for life offers itself as the realistic answer to the realistic question of how man and the world are related to each other."

It is strange how you can meet people, know people for a while, and never discuss really basic issues with them because you can tell where the other stands without asking. When each knows the other's history, why ask rhetorical questions? I have never discussed philosophical issues with Eliot Porter or Brian Davies and they have never sought to discuss them with me. It would have been a silly, incestuous exercise. We just always knew, without verbalizing any of it, that we all belonged to the same faith—"Don't Hurt." There are many roads that lead to that faith—Christianity, Judaism, Islam, the faith of the Hindu, and the philosophy of the Buddhist—but they all get there in the end if each faith is carried through to its logical conclusion. Too many people, most perhaps, never get to where their faith should lead them, to the golden place of "Don't Hurt," because they get hung up along the way with the details —the petty details, really—of the road they have taken.

Brian Davies and Eliot Porter, I believe (although again we have never talked about it and I am perhaps being presumptuous in projecting how they feel in the inner places we have never discussed), have taken their faiths, whatever they may be, and carried them through to the bright places beyond. They don't believe in pain and will not accept it; they don't believe that they can separate themselves from the agony of other creatures and will not try to. Linked as they are, they wonder with Hamlet if we are all to be or not to be and opt for the positive response. That is what these men are all about and what *Seal Song* chronicles.

Preface

by Ray Bradbury

Of Shoes and Ships and Sealing-Wax,
of Harp Seals in the Spring

I would hate to be the captain of a space expedition landing on a strange world confronted
by strange creatures.

I would hate to be the governor of a state making decisions about similar creatures in my
own environment.

I would hate to be President of the United States pleading with other countries to under-
stand our concerns about some warm-blooded animals with whom we share the world.

I would hate to play the Pope's part in such an antagonistic world.

I would hate to be God, pointing here and saying: Procreate. Pointing there and saying:
Leave the room. Forever.

These thoughts crowd in upon me as I leaf through the book and look at the photographs
that you hold in your hands.

If you will permit me random thoughts before I stumble into my inconclusions.

I have often wondered what we might do if, landing upon a far planet, we were confronted with a race of giant spiders, whose architectures of web spanned hundreds of yards instead of measurements of feet and inches. Would we, if we could, invent a very largish boot and step on them?

If, here on Earth, tomorrow, someone said that the black widow was an endangered species, would we care, would we weep, would we move to save?

I ask these questions in no frivolous mood.

These are difficult times, but then they have always been difficult times. We are stuck with an incredible age when we can do everything and because we can do it we must. By everything I mean everything worth doing, everything that, one would hope, we all value. We can give priority to a rainbow of excursions with ideas and outcroppings of those ideas into a real world and the world waiting beyond in the sky.

Which means we can build thresholds on the Moon and Mars and at the same time clean the ice packs of blood for a time and let certain creatures alone for a while and gently pressure the better selves hidden in many men who live in and out of cruel weathers to take some few summers off before picking up the bludgeon again.

I suppose if we carried this pressure far enough, we would knock the sledgehammers out of "ox-killers' hands" in butcher factories and revert to herbivorousness. But the cow is threatened only personally and not as a diminishing race.

So we go with puzzlement and paradox, confused feelings, delayed priorities, other people's necessities, clean and unclean consciences.

Finally, all that I really know is the signal that flashes from the eyes of the creatures within this book. Something of my soul fires itself in that gaze, deny it as I might. And whether it is romantic and fallacious and oversentimental beyond sentiment, I must respond.

In some far part of the Universe, ten thousand years from this noon, we may well confront creatures more vital, more intelligent than ourselves, who will read in our eyes, one hopes, a similar signal. What we want at that moment is recognition. Acceptance. A welcoming in to some universal sill.

And, once in, we would also hope, there is no killing club behind the door.

That about says it. The world, the sea, the land, the sky, the worlds beyond our world, the Universe itself, are filled with miracles both small and large. I stand in terror of some of it, in awe of all of it.

These are not nephews or cousins in this book. But somewhere far back down the line, our hearts and blood moved much the same. Some old racial memory lost in me remembers this. It is hard for me to look and not read the bright signals. I hear that old heartbeat from a million-plus years ago.

Their family, my family, our family, are here gazing at one another in this book. I cannot refuse the stare that asks great questions that must be answered. I cannot turn away.

1 My First Whitecoat

There's no doubt in my mind that the baby harp seal is one of the loveliest creatures on earth. The eyes—dark and inquisitive—captivate you first. Next your attention is drawn to the twitching black button of a nose and the dark stiff whiskers jutting to each side. Then you notice the white coat in which those haunting, liquid eyes seem to be floating. The inch-long hair that covers the young animal's skin looks like an explosion of gossamer, or the white puff of a dandelion. And then, as you linger and watch, all but the eyes and nose of the tiny seal seems gradually to disappear as its body blends into the incredible whiteness of the background.

I saw my first "whitecoat" in March 1965. I was working as an investigator for the New Brunswick Society for the Prevention of Cruelty to Animals when Canadian government officials asked me and two other animal-welfare experts to inspect the annual harp seal hunt in the Gulf of St. Lawrence. Reports of cruelty when the baby seals were clubbed to death had upset many Canadians, and it was our task to see if the slaughter could be made more humane.

The three of us boarded a Sikorsky helicopter on Prince Edward Island and flew for the sea ice. We were eager to see the seals, although we did not look forward to witnessing the killing. As we flew over the Gulf, I looked down on a fantastic wonderland. As far as I could see, huge slabs of ice floated on the ocean in a crazy patchwork pattern. One could imagine that a giant creature had gathered in its hands an enormous puzzle of ice and then scattered the pieces carelessly over the cold, dark water.

Many of the ice floes, or pans as they are often called, were large enough to land on. Our pilot, swooping down low, increased the pitch of the rotor blades to grip the crystal-clear air as he settled us gently on the ice, close to a small herd of harp seals, some fifty miles north of Prince Edward Island. The pan he had chosen was as large as a city block and we had to walk several hundred feet to get to the seals themselves.

The older female seals, at the sight and sound of our helicopter, had crawled to the edge of the pan, where they could slip quickly into the water if threatened. There, warily poised, they waited by leads (which are open-water gaps between the pans) or by seal-sized air holes in the ice that they had kept from freezing over by constantly getting in and out of the water to tend their babies. We could see no live baby seals with the herd, and it was evident from all the blood in the area that the hunt had decimated this group of animals before our arrival. I was not surprised that the seals appeared to be afraid of us.

I crunched and squeaked through two inches of crisp snow to the edge of the ice floe, and where the edges of the pan had been ground against others by the wind and ocean currents, twelve-foot pressure ridges of ice had burst jaggedly upward. The blinding ice field seemed to reach out to infinity and I felt utterly insignificant as I matched myself against that frozen universe.

I filled my lungs with the pure, cold air as my eyes roamed the surface of the ice, absorbing its many shades of white, blue, and green. Peering down into the clear surface water between the floes, I could see blocks of ice up to four feet thick grouped in tumbled formations extending beyond my range of vision into the blackness of the deep sea. Above the water, and in all directions, the ice was a tortured mosaic of snow-covered pressure ridges. I sat down on a bench of ice and was humbled by the beauty of this sub-Arctic seascape framed by an azure sky. The wind murmured and I could feel the heartbeat of the living ocean rocking the pan on which I rested.

Suddenly, out of the corner of my eye, I noticed movement and my spell of solitude was sharply broken. Walking carefully across some loose, broken ice, I came across my first baby harp seal. I was spellbound! The bundle of white fluff appeared about the size of a two-year-old human infant. (I later learned that it was probably about ten days old and weighed some forty pounds.) The seal wriggled toward me, crying all the while and using the nails on its tiny flippers to pull itself along the ice. Then, perhaps sensing that I was not its mother, it stopped, and looked distinctly puzzled. When I did not make any move or sound, it quickly lost interest in me and began to doze on the ice.

After a few moments I slowly edged forward. Eyes snapped open for a brief moment and then the young seal drew its head back into the fat over its little shoulders and stopped breathing. The black eyes closed very tightly and tears squeezed out between long eyelashes. The motionless animal appeared to be in a trance and there was no reaction when I gently touched it. After a minute or two, however, its eyes opened and blinked at me as a wet, black nose flared to fill oxygen-starved lungs with air. Then, with a cry, the little whitecoat twisted and scrambled away from me, making curious tracks in the snow with its tiny flippers and round little body.

By the end of that day I knew that I belonged to the seals, and I decided to learn as much as possible about them. Although I hadn't seen the hunt itself, I had seen its effects, and I knew that I must work as hard as I could to see the slaughter banned forever.

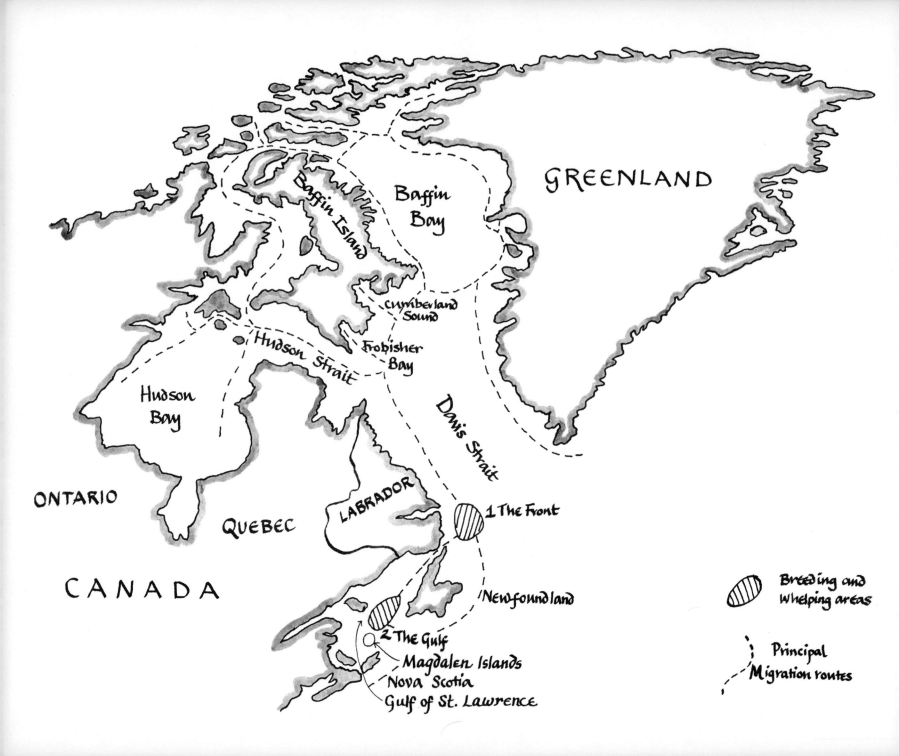

GREENLAND

Baffin
Bay

Baffin Island

Cumberland
Sound

Frobisher
Bay

Hudson Strait

Davis Strait

Hudson
Bay

ONTARIO

LABRADOR

QUEBEC

1 The Front

CANADA

Newfoundland

2 The Gulf
Magdalen Islands
Nova Scotia
Gulf of St. Lawrence

Breeding and
Whelping areas

Principal
Migration routes

2 The Life of the Harp Seal

The northwest Atlantic harp seal population spends most of the year in the food-rich waters between northern Canada and Greenland. Because man cannot exploit the seals much when they are in the northernmost part of their range (which may cover as much as one million square miles along the sub-Arctic coasts) little is known about their activities there. We do know that the seals travel in small groups (or pods), feeding primarily on capelin, a plentiful sardine-sized fish. And that in the fall, as the surface of the ocean freezes, they begin their long migration south along the edge of the advancing winter ice to reach their spring breeding grounds, some two thousand miles away.

The so-called Canadian harp seals breed in two locations: on sea ice off the Magdalen Islands in the center of the Gulf of St. Lawrence (where they are known as the "Gulf" herd), and on the ice floes in the waters off the coast of Labrador/Newfoundland, near Belle Isle (where they are referred to as the "Front" herd). The Gulf pups are born within a few days of each other in early March, while the Front herd whelps a little later. Other harp seal populations are found in the Soviet Union's White Sea, and off the Jan Mayen

Islands, near Iceland, where their numbers have been severely depleted by commercial seal hunters.

During the nursing period in early March the female harp seal is a very attentive mother, rarely leaving her pup for more than half an hour and constantly returning to allow it to nurse. She herself does not feed during this time but lives off her body's reserves of fat. About two and a half weeks after whelping, the female's maternal instincts dwindle, for she is coming into estrus (or "heat"). Soon, in accord with nature's design, she will leave her pup alone on the ice and slip into the water in search of a mate. The male seals, meanwhile, are congregating beneath the ice, and as a receptive female approaches, they scuffle and even fight until one is the winner. The victorious bull will then court his mate tirelessly in and under the water for as long as an hour before breeding.

By April the spring sun has begun to heat the water and air, causing the ice to melt from south to north with the advance of warmer weather. Staying close to the retreating edge of the ice, the adults slowly start their long journey north.

The females are now pregnant again, but each fertilized egg will remain dormant for about twelve weeks so that birth the following spring can coincide with the best possible ice conditions. At this time they may have lost as much as thirty percent of their body weight, since they have eaten little or nothing for weeks and have drawn on their reserves of blubber for milk to feed their babies. (The males will have lost somewhat less weight.) Their normally sleek coats are now a lusterless covering that must be molted before they continue their journey. Lethargically, both males and females pull themselves onto the ice to sleep and molt so that they can enter the water again to start feeding to regain their strength.

The pups have remained alone on the ice. Already they have shed their white natal coats and are now sporting beautiful velvety pelts, gray-blue in color with darker gray markings. At this stage, harp seal pups are called "beaters" by the seal hunters. As beaters, they stay on the ice for as long as a week or so, reluctant to go into the water, but eventually hunger prods them and they begin to move around, at first joining each other gregariously on the ice, and then leaving the melting ice to search for food. When they enter the water for the first time the pups are excited and flustered, indeed rather clumsy. But within a few days they can swim with almost the same skill as the older seals and soon they are feeding ravenously on tiny crustaceans.

From this time on, the day-to-day life of the adolescent seals is something of a mystery since they don't rejoin the adult herd until they are about four years old and approaching sexual maturity. They do, however, head in a northerly direction, though far behind the adults.

At this adolescent stage the seals are called "bedlamers" (a corruption of the French phrase *belle de la mer*, meaning "beautiful one of the sea"). As they mature and experience their first adult molt, a harp-shaped black marking gradually emerges on their silvery-gray backs. It is this marking that earns the harp seal its name. Although the hair coat of the seals looks furry and soft to the touch, it is actually made up of short, stiff hairs a little like a nylon brush. The seals' scientific name, incidentally, is *Pagophilus groenlandicus*, which means "ice lover from Greenland."

A close relative and neighbor of the harp seal is the hooded seal, which gets its name from the loose skin on top of the male's head, which balloons up like a hood when he is under stress. Both harps and hoods are members of the hair seal family and both inhabit the drifting sea ice in the Arctic and sub-Arctic region. Although these two species of seals breed in the same vicinity, I have never seen any interaction between them. Like the harp seals, the hoods have also been hunted for years, but restrictions have now been placed on the hunting of hooded seals in the Gulf, where they are very rare.

The female hoods mature when they are between three and five years old and they breed, like the harps, in the spring. Their babies are born not white all over but with white bellies and blue-gray backs, which account for their nickname, "bluebacks." Hoods are different from harps in several other important ways. They are larger—the male hooded seal can weigh up to a thousand pounds and is generally stronger and more aggressive than the harp male. In fact, the bulls are quite protective of the young and stay close to the females in an "ice nest" during the first part of the nursing period, protecting the mothers and babies against all predators, including man.

Adult seals spend most of their time in the water where the temperature can hover around 30° Fahrenheit (−1.1° Centigrade) and rarely goes higher than 45° F. (7.2° C.), yet they are able to maintain an internal body heat of 98° F. (36.7° C.), thanks to the blubber beneath their skin. Besides providing a protective insulation against the cold, this layer of fat streamlines their bodies and helps buoy them in the water and gives them a reserve of energy when food supplies are low or when they are fasting, as during the whelping and breeding period.

The harp seal is marvelously adapted to its environment. It has no external ear, but a tiny opening a few inches behind the eye enables the seal to hear much as humans do when it is above the surface of the water. Below the surface, water pressure and involuntary muscular action shuts the opening and the seal receives sound waves by conduction through bone and cartilage. The large eyes of the harp seal enable it to see well in the dark waters below the ice, yet above the surface the pupils constrict into tiny slits that allow it to see (although rather nearsightedly) despite the intense glare of the sun. The flippers of the seal are not as efficient for moving on land as the legs of other mammals, but they are superbly designed for swift propulsion through the water. The seal's sharp teeth, which are effective in catching fish, can be dangerous weapons as well. In fact, the easiest way to distinguish a male from a female harp seal is to look for the male's inevitable battle scars earned during the breeding period. It is from the teeth, incidentally, that scientists can determine the age of a seal since dentine is laid down in annual layers.

Although polar bears still offer a threat to the harp seal during the summer and fall months, the bears long ago disappeared—like the walrus—from the eastern shore of Canada, so that the only real threat to the harps in their spring nursery (with the exception of the weather) is the human hunter. Harp seals are capable of living for thirty years in nature, but few of them survive the seal hunt this long.

3 Mother and Baby

Because the seals give birth to their pups on ice rather than on land, the presence or absence of suitable ice is crucial to their survival. But the ice is unpredictable. I have experienced Canadian winters when temperatures were as low as $-36°$ F. ($-38°$ C.), and yet the sea ice was poor. I have also known mild winters with above-freezing temperatures when the ice has been thick. In other words, one never knows exactly what the ice conditions will be from one year to the next—or for that matter, from one day to the next. Indeed, since the floes can move as far as sixty miles in a twenty-four-hour period, conditions can change almost by the hour. When the ice is thin and scattered, pregnant seals have been known to stay in the water holding their pups inside their bodies for as long as two weeks past the usual whelping time, as they search for thick ice that will support them. (Pregnant females may weigh up to four hundred pounds; males are even heavier, weighing as much as five hundred pounds.)

When the females have found suitable ice and whelping is imminent, they haul themselves out of the water and give birth, each female delivering a single white-coated baby. To the best of my knowledge, no one has ever witnessed the birth of a harp seal, although I have seen pups just minutes after birth still splotched with bright red blood. One man told me he had been watching a female seal on the ice and looked away for a few seconds only to find, on turning back, that she had given birth in that brief moment.

The newborn harp seal looks a little bit like a partially deflated elongated balloon. Weighing between fifteen and twenty pounds, the tiny creature has loose folds of yellowish skin covered with fine wool (called a natal coat or larugo) and an outer layer of stiff hairs. Shortly after birth the baby loses this yellow coloration and becomes pure white. The white coat, which makes the infant seal practically invisible against the snow and ice, is a natural protection against predators. Recent studies have concluded, however, that it is more than a camouflage; it also serves as protection against cold temperatures.

According to the Norwegian physiologist Nils Øritsland, the white hair helps the pup to absorb solar energy. "The pup's hair is actually transparent rather than white," Dr. Øritsland maintains. "It transmits the sun's rays down the pelt toward the animal's skin, where they are absorbed as heat. In addition, the hair creates a 'greenhouse' effect, reducing loss of body heat by radiation."

The deflated look of the newborn seal disappears very quickly once it begins nursing, for the female seal's milk—which is converted from the thick layer of blubber beneath her skin—is extremely rich in fat (it has nearly fifteen times the amount of fat found in cow's milk). The young seals nurse frequently during their first two to three weeks, perhaps twenty to thirty times a day, with each meal lasting about five minutes. The whitecoats gain as much as sixty-five pounds during a period of sixteen to eighteen days as they build up their own two-inch-thick layer of blubber. This rapid growth enables them to create a reserve of energy that will not only protect them against the cold, but will also sustain them after the mother seals leave them, and as they learn to fend for themselves.

26

A female seal's two teats are not visible until they extend from her lower abdomen at feeding time. When a mother is ready to feed her pup she will lie on her side and may move the infant toward her teats with a flipper as if encouraging it to nurse. Young seals do not appear to suck while feeding; some experts think the female actually pumps the milk into her baby.

Although normally gregarious, a female seal at whelping time seems to establish a small territory for herself and her pup, and will act aggressively toward other adults and young if they come too close. If a confused pup approaches the wrong mother, it will be angrily driven away, for harp seals steadfastly reject all but their own when it comes time to nurse. Because of the females' discrimination against pups that are not their own, orphaned whitecoats rarely survive, especially if they are less than ten days old and have not built up a reasonably thick layer of blubber on which to live until nature's clock drives them into the water in search of food at three weeks of age.

Returning to the ice after a dive, a harp seal mother appears to follow a standard procedure in searching for her pup among a horde of look-alike infants. First, perhaps because a young seal tends to lie relatively immobile, she always returns to the spot where she left her baby. There, the pup's cry will help her determine its exact location. Once she has found what she thinks is her infant, she sniffs its nose several times, no doubt using scent as a final confirmation. Then, and only then, will she allow the pup to feed.

I find it fascinating that nature has provided each mother with the ability to pick out the sound of her own from the cries of hundreds of whitecoats—for suckling seals almost never stop crying. Actually, scientists have observed that harp seals are much more sensitive to pitch and variation in sound than are humans, and that the individual sound of a seal baby, like its scent, has been imprinted on its mother's brain from the moment of birth.

During the thirteen years that I have been on the ice with the seals I have observed two kinds of temperament in young harps. Some act like opossums when approached: all breathing seems to stop, the nose puckers, the head is pulled back into a thick layer of shoulder blubber, and the eyes close tightly. The only noticeable movement occurs when the nostrils flare as the seal takes an occasional breath. Other pups are more aggressive. Although it seems to be all bluff, they try to intimidate intruders by nipping at the frigid air with toothless gums and scrambling about with a side-to-side wriggle.

Most of the time the baby harp seal eats and sleeps. Whitecoats seem to love basking in the sun, and their movements are usually not more complicated than rolling about to get into a more comfortable position on the ice. During the nursing period the pups normally do not go into the water, except by accident. When this happens, the young seal will quickly scramble back onto the ice to dry out.

Although the baby harp is quite inactive and helpless during the first weeks, its body chemistry is working hard for the future, for the seal must quickly gain weight, that all-important energy reserve it needs to cope with a very harsh environment when the mother leaves to carry on with her adult seal life.

4 Jack and Jill

A few years ago, on returning to Prince Edward Island after filming the seal hunt, I saw children playing games around the small airplanes used to fly hunters to the seals (hunting from the air is now banned). As I watched them playing, I noticed two small white seals lying on the snow. They appeared to be about five days old, and when I inquired, I was told that a pilot had brought them back from the Gulf as playthings for some local children who, quickly tiring of their new toys, had abandoned them.

I knew I had to save the two seals, but calculating my chances of finding their mothers at about one hundred thousand to one (roughly the number of pups born that year), I realized that the Davies family would have to take care of them.

Because of my job with the New Brunswick SPCA, my wife Joan and I had often found ourselves successfully playing parents to many orphaned, abandoned, or injured animals. We had had everything from dogs, cats, baby raccoons, and rabbits to foxes, skunks, porcupines, wild birds, and even a white otter. With all that experience, I thought, a couple of baby seals would be no problem. But, as it turned out, I was very wrong.

I guessed the seals had been without food for at least two days. So, on my way home to Fredericton, New Brunswick, I stopped at an animal shelter operated by the Moncton SPCA to feed my new charges some milk.

With preparations complete, I knelt down on the shelter's kitchen floor and offered one of the seals a baby bottle full of warm cow's milk, expecting it to suck heartily. Two tear-filled eyes looked at me, but the mouth remained firmly closed as the young animal turned its head away to avoid the bottle. The other seal, with what seemed like a gesture of contempt, turned its back on me before I could even begin persuading it to feed. Apparently I did not resemble a fat mother seal.

The answer to the problem of how to feed these stubborn but obviously hungry seals was at my home, one hundred and fifteen miles away. There, I thought, my wife would know what to do. A few hours later I plodded wearily into our living room with a seal under each arm. Joan, a real animal lover, was truly delighted with her new challenge and went straight to the task of trying to feed the two pups.

Calling upon all the resources and skills she had acquired in raising two human babies and dozens of other animals, she tried very hard. But the pair just would not suck on their bottles. They would not lap like kittens or puppies, either, and when we tried pouring milk into their mouths they would not swallow. Indeed, they wouldn't do anything at all but look miserable and hungry. Hours later we gave up and, as it was now the wee hours of the morning, tried to get a little sleep.

We tried all kinds of feeding methods the next morning, but again in vain—and we realized that we had to call for outside help. We discovered that a man who specialized in the esoteric art of raising infant seals might be reached through the Royal Society for the Prevention of Cruelty to Animals in London. Many expensive telephone calls later we finally reached Chief Inspector Charles Morrison of the RSPCA, who told us that baby

30

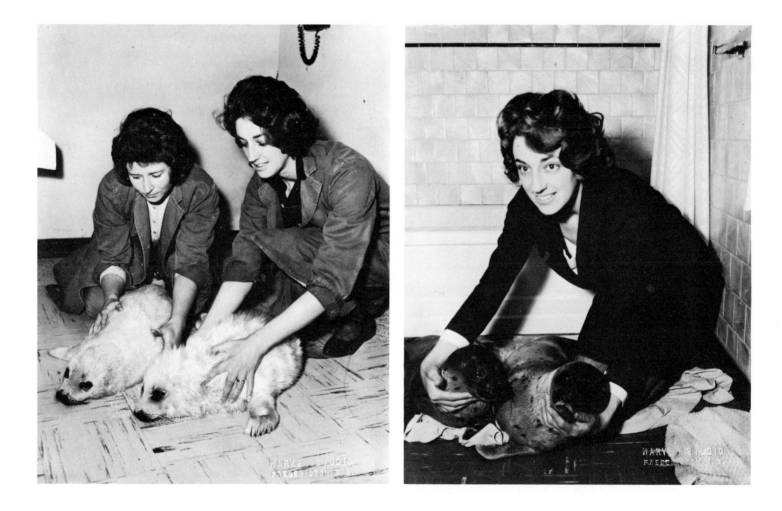

seals will not willingly feed from anything but the nipples of mother seals. "They must be intubated," he said. We found out that this meant pushing a long, thin plastic tube down the throat of each seal directly into its stomach and pouring a liquid diet down the tube. Plain cow's milk, he warned, was not good for harp seals because it was not sufficiently rich in fat. Instead, we would have to devise a special diet with a base of marine oil that they could digest. Now, marine oil was not in abundant supply in our town, but a veterinarian friend, Dr. Elizabeth Simpson, came up with a formula that we hoped would work as a substitute. Jack and Jill, as they were now called since we had finally figured out we had a male and a female on our hands, would be fed with a mixture of butter, milk, and eggs; the mixture was laced with antibiotics to guard against possible infection, since in their undernourished condition the seals were vulnerable to illness.

Elizabeth decided that our seals should be fed at least four times a day, with all equipment sterilized for each feeding. This naturally entailed a lot of work, and we seemed to spend almost all our waking hours feeding the seals or cleaning up after them. The pups were moved into a small unheated room in the basement of our house where we left the single window wide open in an attempt to simulate typical seal living conditions (early spring is rather cold in our part of Canada).

Although Jack and Jill were hardly grateful for our efforts—tubing a seal is uncomfortable for everyone but most of all for the seal—at least we felt that we were getting our formula into the right place. But it wasn't working. They should have been gaining about three pounds a day—which is the appropriate gain in nature—but in fact they were losing weight on our concocted diet. And, in spite of our precautions, Jill became sick with bronchitis and both animals suffered from persistent diarrhea. Without that precious oil, it seemed they might not have much longer to live.

Finding the oil would be difficult enough, but we had no idea how to cope with the considerable costs of purchase and delivery if we did find a source of supply. Happily, this problem was solved when Canadian newspapers ran a United Press International wire story entitled "Got a Dime for a Cup of Oil?" We soon received more than five hundred dollars for the seals, and Jack and Jill became instant celebrities. But our little friends weren't after fame, just a decent meal, and we had to act fast.

Another emergency call to the RSPCA in England brought the promise of the badly needed oil, and hour after hour we waited for its delivery, the tension made worse by the fact that our seals were clearly failing. Much to everyone's relief, a helpful Air Canada employee finally located some oil in London and the airline flew the greasy cans free of charge directly to Fredericton. Within minutes of the shipment's arrival, Jack and Jill were filled with a life-saving meal—and they actually looked contented for the first time since I had picked them up on Prince Edward Island.

But life didn't become any easier for Joan and me. On a typical morning Joan would go down to the basement early. Because Jack and Jill were not toilet trained, they would be practically swimming in a night's collection of droppings. (The heavy odor of harp seal and oil made the house a less-than-desirable environment for us humans.) Joan would wrap each wriggling, squalling twenty-pound seal in one of our few bedspreads and carry them, one at a time, up two flights of stairs to our bathroom, where they would be deposited in a tubful of cold water. Looking exquisitely graceful, they would then splash, dive, and attempt to catch the water as it sprayed from the tap. Toni, my four-year-old daughter, would guard the tub, pushing Jack and Jill back into the water whenever their curiosity took them over the side. On weekends my eight-year-old son, Nicky, would relieve Toni as tub guard. We had become a full-time seal family.

During bath time Joan would mop up the basement floor with the available bedsheets. Next came the germ-killing operation—buckets of hot water, disinfectant, a scrubbing brush, and a good deal of elbow grease would be employed in scouring floors and walls. It would usually be about ten a.m. before the seal-soiled bedspreads and sheets were deposited in our washing machine. And then it was time for the first feeding of the day. While the seal formula was being heated, an assortment of bottles, jugs, spoons, and tubs would be sterilized. Then our bathtub would be emptied, much to the dismay of the two acrobatic seals, who would try to follow the water down the drain.

Before Jack and Jill were fed, they and the "warden of the tub" had to be dried off (and the bathroom cleaned up). Then the seals could eat. Unfortunately, they never seemed to realize that a plastic tube was the harbinger of a full tummy and they always fought the intubation procedure. But eventually they would relax as the warm food flowed into their empty stomachs.

By the time the cleanup from the ten o'clock meal was completed, it always seemed to be just about time for the two p.m. feeding. I usually made it home from work to help with the last two meals of the day—at six and ten p.m. By eleven o'clock at night, Joan and I, both seal-weary, would tumble into our sheetless, bedspreadless bed for a sorely needed rest. There never seemed to be a moment to do anything else during our waking hours but care for seals.

The Jack-and-Jill caper did have its memorable moments. One night we got the seals mixed up at feeding time and Jack received the better part of two dinners. He looked like a fountain as liquid spouted out of his mouth as quickly as we poured it in. Although it was a lot of work, we had lots of moral support during this time. Thanks to the media coverage, people from all over town knew what we were going through and nearly every day someone we had never met before would turn up on the doorstep with a pie, a cake, or a loaf of bread to keep the human part of our family as well nourished as the seals.

But the Davies seal circus couldn't go on forever. After three weeks, when the seals were steadily putting on a pound a day, we made the difficult decision to place them in a zoo. We felt sure that their poor start in life had not properly equipped them to deal with their tough natural environment, and we believed that they would surely die if we put them back into the ocean. And so, in spite of our affection for them, Jack and Jill were sent to a new home—the Vancouver Zoo in British Columbia.

At the zoo the two seals were put on a diet of fish, and at first they did well. But not for long. Sadly, Jack died within six months and Jill after a year. I later discovered that harp seals, for reasons still not completely understood, are almost impossible to raise successfully in captivity. Indeed, the experts felt that Joan, who was the real heroine of it all, had performed a minor miracle by bringing them along as well as she did.

One might wonder whether all the trauma that Jack and Jill were put through was worth it to them. I believe it was. Although life for them was not long, it was as long and as happy as we could make it. And I believe that for seals, as for man, life is almost always preferable to death.

5 Underwater with the Seals

In 1970, I lay flat on the ice and looked down an air hole in one of the pans and saw by chance a magnificent natural aquarium with hundreds of seals gliding around. I decided then and there that I must go beneath the ice and swim with them. At this time I was planning to make a film on the seals for the International Fund for Animal Welfare, and thought that a dive sequence would add a great deal to the film. So, when the film was being made in 1973, I gathered together a team of underwater photographers to accompany me to the ice.

In order to film the seals in their world we made plans to stay with them on the ice—some forty-five miles from land—for three days and two nights. None of us had dived with five-hundred-pound seals before, so we approached this challenging adventure with special care. How would the seals treat us underwater? Would we be considered intruders, or would they accept us?

As we flew out to the Gulf herd I marveled all over again at the familiar sight of adult seals strung like dark, broken necklaces along the edges of the bright pans. Seal tracks in the snow went in all directions, crisscrossing like a railroad yard, and I was glad to be back.

As the time for our dive grew nearer, we became a little apprehensive. This wasn't a swimming pool or a Florida beach, but freezing ocean waters with unknown currents and jagged ledges of dangerous ice. Finally the waiting was over, and it was with a sense of relief that we gingerly put our reluctant bodies into the near-freezing water. As our wetsuits immediately filled with icy water the first shock hit like a hammer, and before we could even think of filming we had to warm this water with our body heat. It was quite a few minutes before we recovered enough to look around us.

On the ice the harp seals are rather awkward and clearly not in their element. Under the ice, however, they are masters of their environment. They swam right up to us, and I could tell from their eyes that they regarded us with curiosity and interest rather than fear or hostility. Free of tension, they seemed perfectly relaxed as they made a close, thorough inspection of the strange-looking creatures who had joined them. Apparently weightless in their water world, they twisted and rolled with grace and ease as if they were performing an underwater ballet just for the benefit of our cameras.

Daylight plunging down through the open leads into the ocean made a myriad of spectacular images: light on ice, light on water. Through the seal-sized air holes in the pans the sunlight shafted downward in pillars of molten gold thrusting into the crystal-clear emerald-green sea. Tiny fragments of ice floating in the near-freezing water reflected the light as though each were a brilliant diamond. When I descended one hundred feet beneath the ice, a depth beyond the reach of light, I swam in velvet-black water feeling as though I were weightless and gliding effortlessly through the cold depths of space.

Sometimes there were as many as a hundred seals in the same area, all keeping a constant vigil on what was happening above and below them, and often checking on their pups through the nearby air holes. On the ice we knew that the air was ringing with the chorus of thousands of seal pups crying for their mothers, but underwater there was only the gurgling of our own escaping air and the background rumble of throaty seal voices.

When a seal made a loud splash as it entered the water it would be joined by several companions and the group would swim in unison, playing and rolling. Often the seals would cluster together just under the water in the leads, then float along the surface, seeming incredibly content with life.

Not only the adult seals go into the water. Back on the surface I had once seen a little pup scramble toward its mother, who was treading water in one of the air holes. The crying pup tried to reach across the hole to touch her with its nose, but suddenly it started to slip and in an instant splashed into the cold water just as its mother dove below the surface. The pup's immediate reaction was to try to get out, but its little flippers were not long enough to reach out of the water to the ice surface. It struggled for a while and I was just about to help it out myself when the mother broke through the water and pushed the pup with her back onto the ice. Apparently none the worse for its dunking, the infant seal was soon nursing contentedly.

A harp seal's underwater acceleration is phenomenal, peaking at about twenty miles per hour. It takes a human about thirty-five seconds to descend eight feet, whereas a seal can dive one hundred feet in as little as fifteen seconds. Often the seals use a tremendous burst of speed when they first dive in, perhaps to reach feeding depth as quickly as they can without dispersing the school of fish they have sighted. Their endurance is equally astonishing. An experienced human free-diver can go down some two hundred feet and hold his breath for about three and a half minutes. But seals can stay underwater for as long as thirty minutes, and it is believed that they can go as deep as six hundred feet. They rise rapidly to the surface at a rate that would cause a human to suffer the bends.

How can the seal accomplish these feats of endurance in the darkness far below the surface? Some researchers (they are called pinnipedologists) at Guelph University in Ontario have been studying this phenomenon and other facts about the harp seal for more than a decade.

The scientists, headed by Dr. Keith Ronald, are attempting to determine how the seal supplies its brain with the oxygen necessary for life during deep dives. Their conclusions include the observation that the seal's blood is twice as rich in hemoglobin (which picks up oxygen from the lungs) as human blood. A huge blood vessel running up the spine of the harp seal takes up about one-third of the space inside the bony structure. This vessel is significantly larger than the aorta, which is the largest blood vessel in most other animals. The harp seal, underwater, is able to shunt blood away from other parts of the body and into this vessel to feed the brain with needed oxygen. Another very unusual characteristic of harps is their ability to reduce their heart rate from as many as one hundred and fifteen beats a minute to ten a minute in order to conserve oxygen in extended dives. Although their lungs are not much larger than ours, their blubber and flexible ribs enable them to withstand water pressure.

The Guelph team is also investigating the seal's ability to hear sounds underwater. A good stereo system can produce between twenty and twenty thousand cycles per second, and a human hears from one hundred to fourteen thousand cycles. But scientists have determined that a harp seal can hear at least one hundred thousand cycles per second.

Other tests are being conducted to determine the relative intelligence of the harp, and responses have been impressive. According to Dr. Ronald, the harp seal has a brain almost as advanced as the dolphin's, which itself is considered to be just behind (or perhaps ahead, depending on how one views these things) of the human brain.

4

5

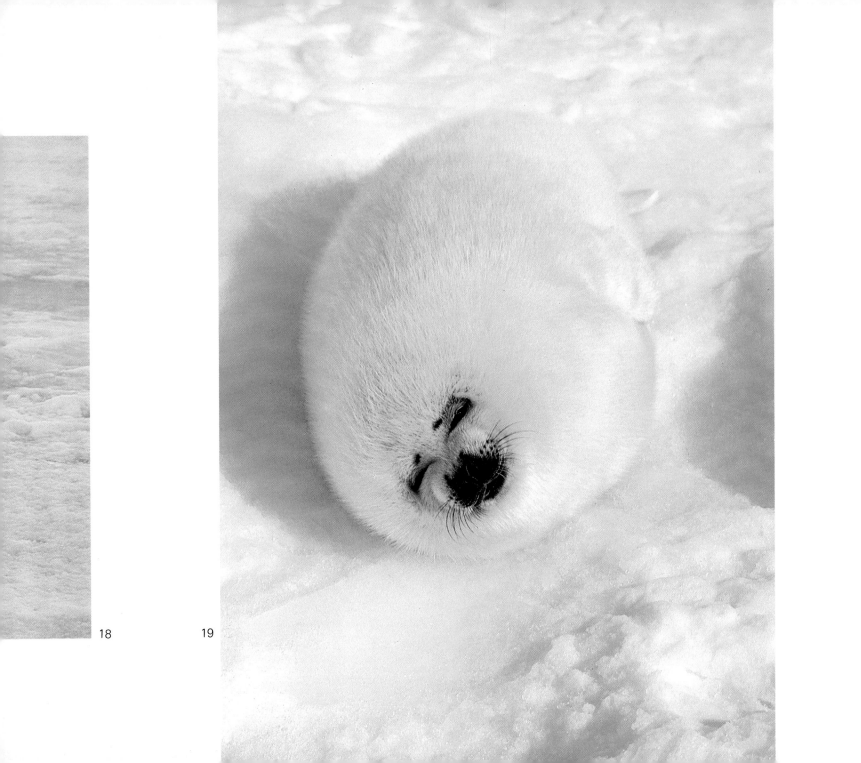

18   19

1. A baby harp seal wet from an inadvertent dunking in the icy water.

2. The Newfoundland coast.

3. The Gulf of St. Lawrence. (Photo by Mark Read)

4–5. The forest in Newfoundland. (#4 photo by Mark Read)

6. The coast of Belle Isle off Newfoundland.

7. Icebergs in the Davis Strait.

8. Harp seals on an ice floe or "pan" surrounded by leads in the Gulf of St. Lawrence.

9. Seals on a large ice floe in the Gulf; the mother seal, in the middle ground, has just emerged from an air hole in the ice to check on her pup.

10–11. Mother harp seals in the Gulf herd.

12–13. Seals underwater in the Gulf of St. Lawrence. (Photos by William Curtsinger)

14–16. Seals in the Gulf herd. Note that the pups are beginning to molt, showing a grayish coloration through the white coat on their foreheads.

17. A baby harp seal enjoying one of his many daily feedings.

18. A mother harp sniffs her pup to make sure she has found the right one.

19. A baby seal in its "play-dead" response to a threat.

20–24. Harp seal pups making themselves comfortable on the ice.

25. A "blueback" or baby hooded seal, which is born with a dark coat on its back and white on its belly.

26–28. Mother seals in the Gulf herd.

29. "Windrows" of snow on pans at the "Front."

30. Thin sea ice—unsuitable for the seals.

31. Broken pans at the "Front."

32. A sealing vessel making its destructive way through a seal nursery.

6 A Fight for Survival

Several years ago, on a gray, overcast day, I flew to the Gulf of St. Lawrence with a Canadian Broadcasting Corporation cameraman to film the harp seal hunt in order to arouse the public to its cruelty. Our helicopter dropped us off about five miles from the Magdalen Islands, near the edge of land-fast ice, and returned to pick up some more observers.

Suddenly the ocean began heaving as the high winds became a gale. We sheltered behind a pressure ridge of ice listening to the wind screaming at seventy miles an hour or more. Then the pan we were standing on broke loose and whirled out to sea. In the near-freezing frenzied waters our small ice raft raced along, twisting and turning, at a speed of maybe ten miles an hour. A ledge of land-fast ice jutted out and we jumped to safety just as the pan we had been on turned upside down. By this time the foaming seas were hammering up loose pieces of ice and tossing them skyward. Where the ice was still connected to the land the huge swells were breaking it up, heaving giant floes into the air to topple and crash into the water or onto other pans.

Reasonably safe ourselves, we stood and watched the seals fight for their lives in the sudden storm. The adults, obviously recognizing the danger, retreated as best they could from the crashing slabs of ice. Then, as the ice settled momentarily, they would quickly scramble back to their pups in order to lead them away from the most dangerous areas. With each new surge of the ocean this brave and dangerous act was repeated and, as we watched helplessly, many mothers and pups were killed in the maelstrom.

But the shifting ice is not the only danger the harp seals face. They are also hunted by man because some people desire the seal's pelt.

Exact figures do not exist but it is estimated that years ago, before seal hunting became big business, harp seals numbered perhaps ten million in the northwest Atlantic. Nowadays the population may be one million; it may be less. The reason, of course, is that man—in his greedy and heedless way—has managed to kill the seals in such quantities that their survival is now, according to many experts, a real question.

Before Europeans settled Newfoundland and Labrador, the Eskimos hunted the seal, using kayaks and nets in order to obtain meat and skins for garments. Later the European settlers employed both nets and guns to take seals. They used the meat for food, seal oil for their lamps and for cooking, and sealskin for clothing. And what they could not use, they sold. Because of the size of the herds the impact of early local hunters had little effect on the harp seal population.

But by 1800 sealing had become a big industry in Newfoundland, employing perhaps half the population in the spring of the year. Using larger boats and more effective weapons, modern sealers have killed perhaps as many as sixty million seals over the last one hundred and seventy-five years—skinning them on the ice and taking the sculps (the skin and underlying layer of blubber) back to shore for processing into leather, fur, and oil. Newfoundland sealers were soon joined by hunters in large wooden sailing vessels from other countries—England, Scotland, Germany, Holland, and Norway—who came in search of whales as well as seals. By the middle of the nineteenth century the annual kill of seals averaged over five hundred thousand; in 1850 it reached the incredible figure of one million.

Although the owners of the boats and the companies made a great deal of money, the hunters themselves made very little, in spite of the fact that they had to work under extremely difficult and dangerous conditions. Over the years many boats were lost in the ice, along with thousands of lives. But the poverty of the men and the challenge of the hunt kept them going.

After working their way to the breeding grounds on the ice, the hunters would use gaffs to crush the skulls of the pups and then remove the sculps along with at least one flipper (a delicacy in Newfoundland). Adult seals would be shot and similarly skinned. Then the sculps were dragged onto a pan, where they would be piled high and transferred to the boats. Such hard, unpleasant, and uncomfortable work required a special kind of courage and strength. Being a sealer was thus considered a true test of manhood (a notion that perseveres to this day), and the hunt became an annual ritual.

In 1895 it became clear that the seal herds were diminishing, for a statute was passed forbidding ships to make second and third trips back to the ice "in order to preserve the seal herds from extinction." By this time the annual catch averaged about three hundred thousand. After World War I the average yearly catch dropped to about two hundred thousand, thanks to the scarcity of ships and the falling prices for seal products. Nevertheless, as recently as 1964 the hunt accounted for the deaths of eighty-five percent of the pups in the Front herd (about one hundred seventy thousand) and about sixty thousand adults.

In 1938 Norwegian sealers, using powerful steam vessels, entered the northwest Atlantic sealing grounds after severely depleting the seals in the White Sea and off the Jan Mayen Islands. Although the onset of World War II caused a substantial reduction in the number of

kills, Norway returned after the war with more ships than ever. In 1951 a record international fleet of twenty-seven ships took two hundred and twenty-eight thousand seals. Seal oil prices dropped in the 1950s, but the catching effort increased because new techniques for tanning seal pelts into furs and leather shifted the emphasis of the hunt from oil to pelts. The Norwegians began to concentrate on young whitecoats, although Newfoundland sealers continued to prefer the larger fat babies for their oil.

In addition to using sophisticated navigation techniques and powerful ships that could push through the ice, modern seal hunting employed the airplane and helicopter. Although the use of aircraft was eventually banned, commercial sealing and local hunting by landsmen continue to this day.

The Canadian government employed biologists and conservationists to study the harp seal population, not in any effort to stop the hunt—for there is considerable political pressure from the sealing industry—but in order to determine the maximum sustainable yield: in other words, the number of seals that may be killed each year without depleting the "stock"! Although the resulting statistics were inconclusive, quotas were set and dates for the hunting season established. (In the eyes of many conservationists these restrictions are far too liberal.)

Even if the hunting of seals were to be stopped today, the harp seal population would be endangered because of human interference. Commercial fishing has already begun to reduce the food species on which the seals depend, and industry and agriculture have polluted the marine environment in which they live. Recently a new peril has been added: the possibility of an oil or natural gas blowout in the waters of the seals' breeding areas. It seems that in the name of "progress" the harp seal will continue to be a victim.

7 Conflict with Seal Hunters

After my experiences in 1965 with the seals and those who kill them, the New Brunswick Society for the Prevention of Cruelty to Animals created the "Save the Seals" Fund. As executive director of the New Brunswick SPCA, I had the job of using the special donations that came from all over the world to make as many people as possible aware of the hunt.

To do this I created a "shuttle" for newsmen between a land base and the commercial seal hunt. We believed that if people in Canada and throughout the world were exposed to the brutal facts of the slaughter, pressure on the government to ban it would become unbearable. Or, failing that, we hoped that worldwide media coverage of the hunt would depress the market for harp seal products and would make it uneconomical for the large ships to continue operating. In 1969 the "Save the Seals" Fund became the International Fund for Animal Welfare (IFAW), and I left the New Brunswick SPCA to become chief executive of IFAW—which helps not only the seals but many other animals as well.

Our shuttle of newsmen to the hunt achieved its purpose, and the killing of baby seals became a stench in the nostrils of the civilized world. The Canadian government's reaction, however, was not to stop the killing but to prevent reporters from witnessing it. In 1975 laws were passed that imposed imprisonment and fines on helicopter pilots who landed newsmen close to the hunt. I was a helicopter pilot by then, flying newsmen in IFAW's Jet Ranger, the *Blue Goose*, to the hunt off the coast of Labrador. And I was the first victim of the Canadian government's "revenge" on the anti-seal-hunt lobby when I was imprisoned and fined for violating the new laws.

In addition to instituting laws that, if respected, effectively ban media coverage of the hunt, the governments of both Canada and Newfoundland allowed the pro-seal-hunt groups to take the law into their own hands at bases that IFAW uses to reach out to the seals. In 1977, when I was operating from both the Magdalen Islands in the Gulf and St. Anthony in Newfoundland, the opposition to my work for the seals reached dangerous levels.

Magdalen Islands

Takeoff with a full load of people in the *Blue Goose* is a demanding task on a warm, still day. Height and speed can be increased only gradually because critical temperature/torque limits must be respected. Although not a common cause of much pilot anxiety (modern helicopters are safe), "low and slow" (as in a fully loaded takeoff) is known to be a somewhat risky business if major mechanical failure occurs, especially if it involves the tail rotor.

In 1977, in Canada's Gulf of St. Lawrence, March 12 was a singularly balmy spring day, just right for the three camera people who had joined me for a flight to photograph rare hooded seals. A full load of human beings forced me to do a low and slow takeoff. As I eased the *Blue Goose* into the air, behind us (where I couldn't see them) angry pro-seal-hunt demonstrators began stoning us with rocks picked up from the side of a dirt road. One of the rocks hit a main blade; others barely missed our vulnerable tail rotor. The experience added a decidedly disagreeable element to the seal issue.

Since the commercial seal hunt from large ice-strengthened ships had been banned for the time being in the Gulf, I was using the Magdalen Islands' town of Grindstone as a base from which to fly daily to film live seals on and under the ice. Although I had spent twelve springs on the Islands, nothing I had experienced in the past had prepared me for this year's shouts, jeers, threats, and red placards proclaiming the virtues of killing baby seals. Whenever I left my hotel an angry mob streamed after me, and on my return for the night they kept a sullen vigil outside, as police guarded the doors.

This attempt to scare IFAW away was an organized effort by local seal hunters to protect the so-called noncommercial landsmen's take of seals. They wanted no pressure for a ban on the landsmen's hunt; they thought a film of the seals at peace on the Gulf ice would stir up such pressure.

With scant regard for civil freedoms, the local mayors, or chief magistrates as they are sometimes called, had met with me and set deadlines for me to leave the Magdalen Islands. The first deadline passed without incident, but when I ignored the second one, the rock throwers showed up.

Actually, March 12 was the day I had planned to leave the Islands anyway, so after taking all the photographs we wanted of the hooded seals, I headed for Newfoundland, where the *Blue Goose* and I were to fly journalists from all over the world to the seal hunt at the Front, scheduled to start off the coast of Labrador on March 15.

Late that afternoon, as I flew over Grindstone, lulled by the slight vibration that is a constant feedback to the helicopter pilot, I looked down with a sense of peace. I was glad I was leaving. The days of unremitting tension in an atmosphere of hatred had been wearing. IFAW's job was done, and I was on my way.

Newfoundland and Labrador

IFAW's base of operation at the Front is the Viking Motel, near St. Anthony, which is at the tip of Newfoundland's Great Northern Peninsula. Eighteen miles from town, the lonely motel sits beside Pistolet Bay on the road to the community's tiny airport.

Flying a low pass over the cluster of buildings before landing on the packed snow between them and the bay, I could see dozens of cars lining the dirt road and hundreds of people, most of them wearing black snowmobile suits, milling around the motel front. It looked ominously like a repeat of the Magdalen Islands incident.

After landing, I climbed out of the *Blue Goose* and the crowd surged forward, sweeping over me like an avalanche. I was taller than most of the pro-seal-hunt demonstrators and my head, projecting above them, became the target for a lot of flying snow, ice, and Newfoundland spit. I tried ducking, but that just provoked some kicks and, for some droll reason, pinches!

I tried making slow progress toward the motel, but the black snowmobile suits soon became so thick that I was forced to stop. Trapped, I faced at point-blank range the business end of a loudspeaker brandished by a Mr. Pilgrim, who proceeded to lecture the world at full volume on the moral turpitude of one Brian Davies and the merits of beating up baby seals.

Deliverance finally came in the form of two perspiring Royal Canadian Mounted Police officers who plucked me from the throng and shepherded me to the motel. There the motel-keeper, Merrill White, met me with coffee and compassion.

Outside in the snow the pro-seal-hunt multitude, vowing that no force on earth could move them, threw a deep picket line around the *Blue Goose* and five other Jet Rangers that IFAW had commissioned to transport newsmen to the hunt. "Brian Davies is definitely grounded!" they loudly proclaimed.

Their purpose was obvious. Keep IFAW on the ground and the journalists would not reach the hunt. Why were they so keen to keep the hunt hidden? If there were no media coverage of the carnage, they believed, there would be no public pressure to end it!

I tested the line of demonstrators on a couple of occasions to see if they meant business. They did. A head count gave odds of three hundred to one in favor of the snowmobile suits. The situation worsened swiftly, and within a few hours the "opposition" controlled virtually the entire motel complex.

At this time there were only some five police officers in St. Anthony, and I was warned by the senior officer that he did not have enough men to guarantee my safety. He pleaded with me not to make further attempts to reach the helicopters and asked me to avoid a confrontation until extra police arrived.

Meanwhile, our captors kept a twenty-four-hour watch over us, refreshing themselves at the motel bar in shifts until, eventually, the police asked that it be closed since tempers were getting dangerously out of hand.

The terms of our captivity depended very much on the mood of the individual demonstrator. Sometimes newsmen were allowed out of the motel complex but were kept away from the helicopters. Other times they were pushed and shoved whenever they tried to exercise freedom of movement.

There were many foreign journalists in the Viking Motel and, angered at events and at the slow response of the police, some of them telephoned their embassies in Ottawa to ask that pressure be put on the Canadian authorities to restore order. Carrying his outrage a step further, Roger Caras of the American ABC television network, contacted the commissioner of the RCMP, demanding protection and freedom of movement for his news team.

When senior RCMP officers in Ottawa took control of the response to our predicament out of the hands of the Newfoundland authorities, events moved quickly. One hundred riot-trained and -equipped police were rushed to St. Anthony and, early on March 15, order was restored. Two and a half days had been lost—and the seal hunt was beginning

As soon as our helicopters were freed, we refueled and rushed the first of forty-five newsmen over the fifty-eight miles of ocean to the hunt scene. There we faced the worst ice conditions I have ever encountered.

The sea spread around us like pebbly linoleum, with chalky ice patches embedded in what seemed to be green ice. But it was clear that the matrix wasn't ice at all. It was a deadly slush. The whole mess heaved on twelve- to sixteen-foot swells. The ice floes washed back and forth, and the gaps between them, opening and closing, were an instant corridor to death.

For days I ferried newsmen to and from the killing, and world media coverage of the massacre exceeded by far anything IFAW had been able to organize in the past. Reporters and photographers from the *Chicago Tribune* and *The New York Times* in the United States, Britain's *Daily Mail*, Canada's *Sun*, from the French magazine *Paris Match* and the German magazine *Quick*, from television and radio networks in the United States, Canada, Norway, Holland, France, Australia, Denmark, Sweden, and other countries—were all there. I believe the 1977 seal hunt was the most heavily documented welfare/conservation event of all time. If there is a better way to stop the slaughter, I don't know what it is.

We are engaged in a battle of attrition with the Canadian authorities and the sealing industry. I can write with conviction that if IFAW gives up, the killing will go on until either the last seal pup dies or another dedicated organization perseveres until the hunt it banned. But we don't plan to give up. On the contrary, IFAW plans to increase its level of activity on a monthly basis so that, month by month, the facts of the hunt will become more embarrassing to the governments involved and damaging to the market price of harp seal products.

8 Pros and Cons of the Seal Hunt

Can the hunt be justified? Canada's Prime Minister Pierre Elliott Trudeau and his government think so. Let's take a look at some of their arguments as outlined in official "Background Documents."

(1) **"The hunt contributes 5.5 million dollars to the Atlantic (mainly Newfoundland) economy."**

Maybe so, but I doubt it. Actually, *Canada 76,* the 1976 edition of an annual handbook published by the Minister of Industry, Trade, and Commerce, lists the total value of hair (harp) seal products for the calendar year 1973–74 as $1,789,748 and the average pelt value to the producer (hunter) as $13.71. My knowledge of the industry leads me to believe these figures. And they are nothing like 5.5 million dollars! Average pelt value would have to rise to about $35 to support such a claim—and so far it hasn't. Indeed, industry spokesmen claim that pelt prices have generally fallen since 1974.

In any event, given the fact that Canada's gross national product is 214.7 billion dollars, the government could surely find other work for the two hundred men employed for four weeks a year in the commercial seal hunt. Surely no sane man *wants* to spend weeks at a time beating baby seals to death. The truth, in my opinion, is that the seals and men suffer because Prime Minister Trudeau has abandoned Newfoundland to a Stone Age economy.

(2) "The 1978 quota of 180,000 is intended to permit a continued increase in the harp-seal population."

The esteemed International Union for the Conservation of Nature and Natural Resources (IUCN) doesn't agree and communicated its concern to the Canadian Minister of Fisheries before the 1978 hunt. "If this year's hunt cannot be called off or delayed," wrote the IUCN, "then the 1978 quota of 180,000 should be reduced to bring it into line with the best scientific findings—and the 1979 hunt should be postponed or cancelled." Interestingly, the chairman of the IUCN's Seal Committee, which drafted the message to Canada, is Dr. Keith Ronald of Guelph University. Dr. Ronald is also chairman of the Canadian government's own (and oft ignored) Advisory Committee on Seals and Sealing.

I'll let Dr. David M. Lavigne, also of Guelph University, have the last word: "The International Whaling Commission [IWC] introduced its New Management Policy [NMP] in 1974. This NMP is still being criticized by many as not satisfying the criteria of a conservative management policy. Nevertheless, if applied to the harp seal, the NMP would dramatically alter the present management scheme. In fact, if harp seals were whales, they would be totally protected at this time."

(3) **"The seal hunt, by Canadians, is the most regulated animal activity in North America, or even the world."**

Wrong! The government's seal protection regulations have been in effect in their present form since 1966. In the twelve years up to 1977, although some two million seals were killed, *not one sealer had been charged under the anti-cruelty sections of the regulations.* In fact, the regulations have mainly been used to prosecute helicopter pilots for flying anti-seal-hunt protesters and newsmen to the killing area.

In my opinion, the regulations are designed to hide the heartless slaughter from the eyes of the world and, as far as the seals are concerned (given the obvious lack of enforcement), are not worth the paper they are written on.

(4) **"The harp seal has a skull plate which is thinner and softer than that found in most mammalian species. It is paper thin, thereby making the method of stunning the seal humanely acceptable."**

Wrong again—according to the distinguished veterinarian and university lecturer Dr. William Jordan, who observed the 1978 hunt for Britain's Royal Society for the Prevention of Cruelty to Animals.

Dr. Jordan found that far from being "paper thin," the skull of a baby seal is well developed and, especially when protected by a thick layer of blubber and skin, hard to crack. He actually found sealers who suffered tendonitis from their efforts with the club.

In contradiction to government claims that all skulls are crushed, he found on his first day on the ice (and the only day he felt he was unnoticed and was working with a genuine sample) that six out of thirteen postmortems revealed intact skulls. In these cases the animal had been hit on the nose or behind the head. He also observed that there were sealers going around crushing with their heels or clubs any skull still intact on the ice after skinning. He saw many instances of mother seals attempting, albeit briefly, to defend their young from the hunters, and returning to carcasses when the men had left.

Dr. Jordan said it appeared to him impossible for the few fisheries officers he saw out on the ice to keep an eye on each sealer to ensure that the slaughter regulations were being obeyed.

(5) "The fact is that if the seal is not kept in balance, then a real commercial fishery is affected, protein food for the international world—the world is affected—and then people genuinely suffer." (Premier Frank Moores of Newfoundland)

Dr. D. E. Sergeant, senior scientist and harp seal specialist at Canada's Fisheries and Marine Service, doesn't agree. He says, "Natural predators do not affect the stocks of prey. Prey affect the stocks of predators. So harp seals do not affect fish stocks, but vice versa."

At least the Canadian government isn't fooling Canadians, as shown by an independent opinion poll taken in Canada in 1978 by the country's largest-circulation publication, *Weekend Magazine*. Its findings were that fifty-seven percent of Canadians want to ban the hunting of baby seals. Only twenty-four percent think the hunt should continue; eighteen percent are undecided; one percent state no opinion. "What's clear," claims *Weekend Magazine*, "is that most Canadians oppose the hunt."

But let's give the last word to the Canadian bureaucrats. Dr. Arthur May, senior spokesman for the Canadian Department of Fisheries, said in late 1976, at a press conference, "We consider the seals the same as seaweed—a marine resource to be harvested."

It has not been easy to convey to the Eskimo mind the meaning of the Oriental similes of the Bible. Thus the Lamb of God had to be translated kotik or young seal. This animal, with its perfect whiteness as it lies in its cradle of ice, its gentle, helpless nature, and its pathetic innocent eyes, is probably as apt a substitute, however, as nature offers.

DR. WILFRED T. GRENFELL,
medical missionary to Labrador, 1909

Epilogue

During the million or so years that seals have existed they have become part of man's mythology and literature. Francis James Child, a professor at Harvard, discovered some years ago an ancient ballad called "The Great Silkie of Sule Skerrie," which has since been recorded by Joan Baez, among others. This ballad is about a seal who swims in the ocean and is transformed into a man when he comes ashore. The seal-turned-man seduces a maid and they have a son whom the father takes with him into the sea when the time comes for the boy to learn to be a seal. Before leaving, the father predicts that the woman will forget them and will marry a hunter who will destroy him and his son:

> *An it sall come to pass on a simmer's day*
> *When the sin shines het on evera stane*
> *Than I will tak my little young son*
> *An teach him for to swim the faem*
> *An thu sall marry a proud gunner*
> *An a proud gunner I'm sure he'll be*
> *An the very first schot that ere he schoots*
> *He'll schoot baith my young son and me.*

The father then gives the woman some gold as a parting present, which she eventually uses to buy her new husband a gun. And, as the man-turned-seal had predicted, the gunner does kill both father and son.

I don't know whether this ballad embodies a longtime folklore tradition, but I do know that my wife's grandfather, an English fisherman, believed, like his father and grandfather before him, that seals were the souls of drowned fishermen. For that reason he would never take part in the hunting of seals. I don't take these fishermen's beliefs literally myself, but I do feel strongly that there is a stronger bond between man and the seal than we now recognize.

One day I suppose we will be able to communicate with some other animals as freely as you and I are now doing through the medium of these written words. If, through some miracle, this were to happen today, I believe that those of us who listened to the seals would hear a story to break our hearts.

Almost all my life I have shared my home with animals and each and every one has been a distinct and fascinating individual. Whatever the species, they have been able to communicate to me emotions that I believe are essentially similar to those that I feel myself.

And why not? It is likely that we all originate from the same vital source and that each evolving life form has had to struggle for survival with the same fundamental environmental stresses. We all have a great deal in common.

Too often we ignore this and treat other animals as if their flesh were somehow insensitive to pain, as though fear were limited to the human experience. Most of us give no thought to the obvious value of pain and fear for the survival of many slow-breeding species. And our ignorance is never challenged by an animal's being able to say, "That hurts me," or "I am frightened."

Unthinkingly, we exploit animals in many ways—in the name of science, food, companionship, and whatever else we feel is necessary to our own survival or comfort. We do awful things to animals, but the worst that we do, it seems to me, is to kill them for the sake of luxury and novelty. This is why I believe the seal hunt is a tragedy that should fill us all with shame.

One day, as we become more sensitive to our fellow travelers in time and space, I believe that the demands of civilized people will end the hunt. Then I will be able to travel to the ice out of love, not out of fear for my friends, the harp seals.